Pigeons

Pígeons

by Dorothy Hinshaw Patent
Photographs by William Muñoz

Clarion Books

New York

For City Kids
—D. H. P.

For all the fond memories growing up
—W. M.

The author and photographer wish to thank Myron Berger, Mark Dunn, Daniel and Daley Hall, Ken Hardman, Alan Harriman, and Corey Richwine, as well as the Art Institute of Chicago, for their help with this book.

Clarion Books
a Houghton Mifflin Company imprint
215 Park Avenue South, New York, NY 10003

Text copyright © 1997 by Dorothy Hinshaw Patent
Photographs copyright © 1997 by William Muñoz

The text is set in 15/20 Garamond.

For information about this and other Houghton Mifflin
trade and reference books and multimedia products, visit
The Bookstore at Houghton Mifflin on the World Wide Web
at (http://www.hmco.com/trade/).

Printed in Singapore

Library of Congress Cataloging-in-Publication Data
Patent, Dorothy Hinshaw.
Pigeons / Dorothy Hinshaw Patent; photographs by William Muñoz.
p.   cm
Includes glossary and index.
Summary: Describes the physical characteristics, behavior,
and usefulness of these birds, which have lived with
people since prehistoric times.
ISBN 0-395-69848-0
1. Pigeons—Juvenile literature.   [1. Pigeons]   I. Muñoz, William ill.
II. Title.
QL696.C63P38   1997
598.6'5—dc20
96–42072   CIP
AC
TWP   10 9 8 7 6 5 4 3 2 1

Contents

Pigeons are completely at home in cities.

Introduction

PIGEONS LIVE JUST ABOUT everywhere people do. Even in the deepest skyscraper canyon, pigeons make themselves at home, perching on fountains and pecking at sidewalks for food. Many city dwellers dislike pigeons, often referring to them as nothing more than feathered rats. Pigeons may be messy, but they have something important to offer anyone interested in nature and wildlife—an opportunity to observe, without traveling to faraway places, how wild animals live.

Pigeons are very tolerant of the humans with whom they share their homes.

Pigeons hardly seem wild—sometimes you almost have to kick them out of your way. But just like wild animals living in the forest or desert, pigeons have to find food, water, and shelter, and they must do what they can to avoid becoming food for other animals, such as cats and peregrine falcons. They need to find mates in the spring, and they build nests and raise their young, just as any wild bird does.

The phrase "bird brain" is used as an insult, but we now know that birds are not stupid at all. Pigeons have shown themselves to be quick to learn and quite intelligent. Intelligence makes sense for pigeons—in order to survive in the many different environments where they live, they have to be adaptable.

Pigeons over time also have had special relationships with people. In ancient times, this gentle bird was a symbol of goddesses like the Greek Aphrodite,

Many people enjoy the companionship of pigeons.

the Goddess of Love. The easily tamed pigeon has served as a pet to millions of people through the ages. No one knows when or where the first pigeons were domesticated (tamed, brought into captivity, and bred especially for certain traits), but pigeons have served humans for thousands of years.

During wartime, pigeons have saved the lives of countless soldiers by delivering vital messages from the front lines to the command posts. With modern communications, the role of the pigeon as a messenger has just about disappeared. But their ability to navigate precisely and to fly quickly has kept pigeons working for hobbyists who race their birds in competition. Today, pigeons are important for many kinds of scientific study in addition to their use in investigations of intelligence and animal navigation. Studies of genetics, hormones, and nutrition have all involved pigeons as important subjects.

*The adaptable pigeon can make its home just about anywhere,
including in this zoo exhibit of an African crowned crane.*

Pigeons are a familiar sight on rooftops.

CHAPTER 1

Pigeons as Birds

THE FAMILIAR CITY PIGEON is actually not a native of North America. The pigeons we know are the descendants of domesticated pigeons that got away and succeeded in living on their own. Animals that escape from captivity and become wild are called *feral*. The "wild" horses that live in the American West, for example, are not really wild— they are feral descendants of horses that were once captive.

The domesticated pigeon originated with the rock dove (*Columba livia*), a species that once lived wild through much of Europe, Asia, and northern Africa. Today, wild rock doves are absent from most of

Like their ancestors, pigeons feel at home among the rocks, here at a zoo.

Europe, even though their feral pigeon relatives thrive in European cities.

Pigeons have lived with people since prehistoric times. They were the very first domesticated birds, tamed by humans from five to ten thousand years ago. At first, people probably collected young pigeons from their nests in caves and fed them until they were big enough to eat. Eventually, humans learned how to raise the birds to adulthood and got them to nest in captivity. In addition, wild rock doves probably settled on their own in the early cities of the Near East. The stone and mud walls of the houses were very much like the rocky cliffs and caves where the birds lived wild, so pigeons easily felt at home there. The grains the people grew made perfect pigeon food, allowing the birds to breed more often than in the wild, since abundant food was available over a broad season. Pigeons that settled in cities also faced less danger from wild predators that were reluctant to enter a town.

The Pigeon Family

Pigeons and doves belong to a family of birds found on every continent except Antarctica. Usually, smaller

The yellow-breasted fruit dove shows the short neck and small head typical of pigeons and doves.

species are called doves while the larger ones are known as pigeons. All together, there are almost three hundred different kinds, or species, of doves and pigeons. Most live in the tropics. These broad-shouldered birds have short necks and small heads. Most pigeons and doves eat small seeds and fruit. Their

(Below left) *The cere is especially obvious on domesticated pigeons.*

(Below right) *When a pigeon, like this jambu fruit dove, perches, three toes on each foot grip the front of the branch while the fourth hangs on to the back.*

The nicobar pigeon is especially attractive, with its mantle of glossy blue feathers.

beaks are straight and rather narrow. A layer of skin, called the *cere*, grows over part of the upper half of the beak. The nostrils open through the cere. A pigeon's sturdy legs end in feet with four toes each. The feathers are varied in color, often with irridescent patches like those on the necks of feral pigeons.

The males court females by strutting in front of them, feathers puffed out, while cooing. The young

The closest pigeon is drinking from a small pit in the paving.

are completely dependent on their parents, who feed them a special milky liquid the parents regurgitate. Unlike other birds that take water in sips and raise their heads to swallow, pigeons and doves immerse their beaks in water and suck up as much as they need without lifting their heads.

The Wild Rock Dove

This ancestor of both domesticated and feral pigeons still lives wild over much of its old range, especially in parts of Asia and on North European islands. It looks much like many feral pigeons—basically gray in color, with orangish eyes, red feet, two black bars on the wings, and iridescent green and purple feathers on the neck.

The rock dove was a natural for domestication. Scientists believe it originated in dry, treeless areas with cliff ledges and caves for roosting and nesting and open country for feeding. Thousands of years ago, humans created a new habitat for rock doves when they began growing crops. As agriculture spread, so did the rock doves, following human farmers and the free grain they provided wherever they

The mourning dove is a native wild species that lives in North America.

settled. Many populations of wild rock doves today are dependent on agriculture for survival.

Rock doves feed mostly on seeds, so grain that has escaped the harvest is perfect food for them. They also eat some small land snails, berries, and perhaps small insects. Like city pigeons, rock doves feed on the ground, walking about and pecking at the surface. It would be difficult for them to feed in deep grass or shrubbery. In addition to idle grain fields, pastures with grass closely cropped by grazing sheep and other domesticated animals make good feeding grounds for rock doves.

Pigeons are adapted to feeding among short grasses on the ground.

Like most birds that live in areas with a temperate climate, rock doves nest in the springtime. They choose sheltered ledges or holes in cliffs and caves, preferring to nest in semi-darkness. Each female lays two white eggs, which hatch in seventeen to eighteen days. Rock doves can produce more than one brood each year.

The Domesticated Pigeon

Throughout the thousands of years that pigeons have lived with humans, more than two hundred breeds have been developed, each with its own purpose. Within each breed, there can be over a hundred different color and marking varieties.

A Birmingham Roller.

A White King pigeon, a large breed developed for eating.

Large birds, such as White Kings and Giant Runts, were bred to produce squabs for eating. An adult runt can weigh over 3.5 pounds, compared with a typical pigeon, which usually weighs under one pound. Flying speed and homing ability were selected to create the racing homing pigeon. Breeds such as Rollers are bred for strange flight patterns. Rollers and the closely related Tumblers do backward somersaults in the sky over a distance of about thirty feet. Rollers can also do forward somersaults. They often are worked in groups of twenty or more, for when one begins to roll, the others will join in, filling the air with somersaulting birds.

Dozens of breeds have been developed for their appearance. Fantails, for example, sport graceful tails

Many domesticated breeds have feathers on their feet and legs.

Breeds like these Short-Faced Helmets can't feed their own young.

that are held upright. Instead of the normal twelve to fourteen tail feathers, fantails have as many as forty-two. Jacobins have a collar of feathers that cloaks the head. A number of pigeon breeds have feathers on their legs that extend over the feet onto the ground. Some breeds have special features that interfere with their natural biology. Short-faced breeds, for example, have small beaks and can't feed their own offspring.

An important part of keeping domesticated pigeons has always been the love people feel toward these beautiful and interesting birds. As a pigeon fancier named Robert Fulton put it, "No one feels surprised that men should love flowers. Some of us can not have flowers; some of us want more return than flowers can give. We would have their beauty; but we crave for an eye that can meet us, a pet that will welcome our approach and show that our regular visit is a joy to both. . . . To the true fancier his pigeons are just such beautiful, rare, *living flowers.*"

The Feral Pigeon

The feral pigeon is an especially interesting bird, for it is so variable. No one knows just how this familiar bird originated in all the different places where it is found. The feral pigeon is a mixture for sure—a combination of wild rock doves that moved into cities in Europe and Asia and domesticated pigeons that escaped from captivity. In each area, different kinds of pigeons could have escaped. While many feral pigeons are gray like their wild ancestors, a flock is likely to include individuals with splashes of white, reddish brown, or black. In Hawaii, most feral pigeons are white, while in many European cities, most are black.

Many color patterns can be seen in a typical flock of feral pigeons.

Feral pigeons differ from rock doves in sometimes subtle ways. Their bodies tend to be narrower, with longer tails, and their bills are generally broader, with larger ceres. But where both are found, an observer

Pigeons live in cities around the world, including in Estonia, where this Soviet-era army officer feeds them.

might be hard-pressed to tell them apart. Because domesticated pigeons were selected for the ability to breed often, feral pigeons are often able to produce more broods of young in a year when food is abundant than rock doves.

Feral pigeons live in cities around the world, surviving in such harsh environments as Ushuaia, Argentina, the southernmost town in the world, very close to the Antarctic Circle, and in numerous locations within the Arctic Circle and the tropics. The climates in such places are very different from the dry, temperate areas where the rock dove evolved. But the shelter and food humans provide make life for the feral city pigeon possible.

Despite their different histories and lives, wild rock doves, domesticated pigeons, and feral pigeons share the same basic behavior and way of life. In this book, the word *pigeon* will refer in general to all three, when behavior is described.

CHAPTER 2

Pigeon Intelligence

SCIENTISTS HAVE COME TO RESPECT the intelligence of pigeons, both through laboratory experiments and by studying feral pigeons. We generally associate the idea of intelligence with a large brain. But the amount of "smarts" crammed into the tiny pigeon skull is truly remarkable.

Studying City Pigeons

Pigeons learn quickly, and they can learn by watching one another's behavior. Louis Lefebvre at McGill University in Montreal, Canada, has studied city pigeons for years and is impressed by their learning

Feral pigeons, like these in Chicago feeding in front of a Picasso sculpture, make excellent subjects for study.

ability. Once, Dr. Lefebvre captured four feral pigeons and trained them to peck through the paper covering over a container of seed. Then he released the birds and set out covered seed containers. Within a month, twenty-four other birds had learned how to get at the food, just by watching the behavior of the trained birds.

City pigeons also can figure out quickly how to get the best food supply. When Dr. Lefebvre and a colleague scattered bread crumbs for the birds, one every ten seconds and the other every five seconds, the birds figured out within moments where the most food was, and two-thirds of them stayed around the researcher who was tossing out crumbs the fastest. Pigeons know where and when people with bags of bread crumbs or bird seed will appear, and they recognize the people who feed them regularly, flocking eagerly to their feet. They also know the sources of water in their neighborhood. I remember once walking through a park in Washington, D.C., where a drinking fountain was left on, and a pigeon was perched on the spout, its beak sucking water from the arching flow.

Pigeons in the Laboratory

While Dr. Lefebvre studies feral pigeons, other scientists prefer the more precise conditions of laboratory research to investigate pigeon intelligence. In the process, they have found out that these small-brained creatures have impressive memories and an amazing ability to categorize objects and to make subtle visual distinctions.

Humans can have trouble remembering the simplest things—locker combinations, phone numbers, people's names. But a laboratory pigeon can learn to recognize 320 randomly chosen photographic slides and can remember 160 slides for two years or more.

Scientists at Harvard University decided to see if pigeons could also recognize concepts and use that knowledge to obtain food. They trained pigeons to respond to slides with different sorts of images. For example, four birds were shown forty slides of all sorts of trees—leafy trees and evergreens, bare winter trees and lush green summer ones. Sometimes the trees stood out obviously from the background. In other slides, the trees were just a part of the background. The tree slides were mixed in with forty other slides with no trees. These slides were chosen to be as much like the others as possible, except for the missing trees.

Each bird had a key in front of it when it was shown the slides. If the bird pecked at the key when a tree slide was shown, it might get a food pellet. If no tree showed in the slide, the bird got no pellet. The slides were mixed up randomly each time they

(Above) *Pigeons can easily tell that both these yellow-leafed birches and . . .*

(Below) *these silhouetted pines are trees.*

were shown. By the second session, three of the birds had already figured out that they should peck when the slide showed trees, and the fourth bird caught on by the fifth session.

At this point, the scientists didn't know if the birds could recognize trees or if their excellent memories were at work. So, they performed another experiment to rule out memory. This time, they used eighty slides of underwater scenes, half with fish and half without. Some of the slides without fish did have a diver, turtle, or other living thing in them. The scientists used two groups of pigeons. One group was rewarded for recognizing fish, just as in the tree experiment. The other group got food pellets for pecking when particular slides appeared. Some of the rewarded slides had fish and some didn't, so those pigeons had to memorize which slides might bring them a pellet. The results of the experiment were clear: birds trained to respond to the concept of "fish" learned twice as fast as the group that had to memorize the slides.

The Harvard scientists continued with more experiments, finding out in the process that just one example of a particular visual concept, such as a leaf from one kind of tree, was all it took for the birds to recognize a concept. Japanese scientists followed up this work by showing pigeons slides of paintings by the artists Claude Monet and Pablo Picasso. After about twenty sessions, the birds were pecking correctly around 90 percent of the time. Then the researchers tried something else. They showed the pigeons new slides, but not just those of Monet and Picasso. Monet was an impressionist painter, while Picasso was a cubist. So the scientists chose additional slides from

(Below left) *Pigeons could tell that this painting by Renoir,* Two Little Circus Girls, *was painted by an Impressionist.*

(Below right) *They would also recognize this Braque painting,* Normandy Harbor, *as cubist.*

the impressionist Renoir and the cubist Braque. The birds trained to peck at Monet pecked at both new Monet paintings and those of Renoir, while the Picasso-trained birds chose Braques as well as new Picassos. The pigeons had learned to recognize elements of the two different painting styles that humans call "cubist" and "impressionist," and all with their little "bird brains."

CHAPTER 3

The Life of Feral Pigeons

PIGEONS ARE VERY ADAPTABLE BIRDS—that's part of their secret of success. They can live in cities or the countryside. While seeds are their preferred food, they will also eat small insects and crumbs. They are perfectly capable of living together in pairs, but usually pigeons tend to roost and feed in flocks.

Pigeon Flocks

A flock provides the advantage of many pairs of eyes and ears alert to predators such as falcons. When a predator threatens a flock, the birds take flight with a loud clatter of wings. The flock sticks together, veer-

Pigeons, like these bathers, spend most of their time in flocks.

ing first one way, then another to avoid the predator. It's very difficult for a falcon to pick one bird out of a flock and attack it successfully.

Like many wild animals, city pigeons tend to feed mostly in the early morning and the late afternoon. A flock of pigeons may always look pretty much the same to us. But actually, even when there is a reliable food source in a particular area, about a third of the birds will be visitors from another part of the city. In this way, pigeons are often checking out possible new food supplies in case a regular one dries up.

When a flock of pigeons encounters a mixture of seeds, each bird specializes in one type. That way, it can focus its pecks on a particular size, color, and shape of particle, allowing it to fill up as fast as possible. The pigeon doesn't swallow the food immediately. Instead, food is stored in a special widening of the esophagus called the *crop*. This behavior also helps the flock, for birds feeding on different kinds of seeds aren't competing with one another. Speed is what counts—the birds don't battle over food. Instead, each gobbles down its chosen food as fast as possible.

After feeding, the pigeons return to their resting places, where they relax, clean their feathers, and sun bathe. As a pigeon rests, the food in its crop gradually moves into the gizzard. The walls of the gizzard are muscular and tough. In the gizzard, sharp bits of gravel grind the seeds into a thick porridge for digestion.

Having a Family

Any city dweller has seen evidence of pigeons' love life. Almost any time a flock of pigeons walks about on the sidewalk pecking up bits of food, at least one male bird will be trying to impress a female. He puffs out his neck feathers so they gleam in the sunlight, and he coos softly as he struts about. The females are just as likely to ignore him as to pay attention. A female needs to choose her mate carefully, as most pigeons mate for life. The male she chooses is likely to remain her companion and fellow parent to all the offspring she produces during her lifetime.

A male pigeon courts a female.

A pair of pigeons bill and coo.

Finding a Mate

Before he begins to look for a mate, a male pigeon finds a place to build a nest and claims a small area around it as his territory. He calls from his territory to attract a female. If another bird comes near, the male doesn't know at first if it is a female or another male, so he acts aggressively. Another male will return the aggression and be chased off, but a female ready to mate won't. The male then sings and dances around the female, lifting his wings, spreading his tail, and inflating his throat as he coos and struts.

If the female continues to watch, the male moves closer and nibbles at her neck feathers with his beak. If she returns the favor, the birds are well on their way to forming a pair and beginning a family. As courtship continues, the male shows his new mate the nesting site. This early courtship may occur over a period of two or three days, interrupted by the ordinary life activities of feeding and resting. Whenever courtship is resumed, it begins again with the bowing and cooing routine of the male.

During the next phase of courtship, the female begs for food from the male, and he responds by opening his bill and letting her insert her bill into his mouth. This behavior is similar to the way the adults feed their young. After the birds have been courting for a week or more, they finally will mate during one of the bouts of "feeding."

Five to seven days after the pair has begun mating behavior, they build their nest. The female sits on the nest site while the male flies off in search of nesting material. He brings it to her, and she tucks it in around her body, building a nest that just suits her. A pigeon nest is often a delicate affair; in cities, material may be hard to find. Pigeons use whatever they can locate

A pigeon nest often consists of little more than a few bits of straw.

nearby to build their flimsy nest—straw, twigs, and feathers are the usual materials.

Once a pair is mated, they spend their time together. When the female flies, the male joins her and will chase away other males that may come near. Together, the birds defend their nesting territory and spend the night roosting together in the nest.

Throughout the life of the pair, the two birds periodically court, with the male strutting around and the female begging for food. The two birds appear to be very affectionate with each other, rubbing their necks together, billing, and cooing.

A mated pair roosts together.

Raising a Family

One of the frustrations for someone wanting to observe pigeon behavior in the city is the difficulty of finding a nest to watch. Hundreds to thousands of birds may live in the city, but locating even one nest can be a challenge. Pigeons generally don't nest out in the open. They choose dark, hidden spots for their nests, such as the spaces between buildings, inside attics, or air shafts. Remember, wild rock doves nest inside caves, so it should be no surprise that feral pigeons seek out dark, quiet places to raise their young. Because pigeons usually nest in colonies, even if many pigeons live in a particular area, they may all be nesting in one attic or old loft. Some pairs do, however, nest alone, so high-rise windowsills may end up being home for a pair of nesting pigeons.

The female pigeon lays her first egg two or three days after the nest is completed. The second follows about two days later. Only rarely are more than two eggs laid. Once both eggs are in the nest, the parents take turns sitting on them. The eggs must be kept warm to develop properly. Each parent has a special *incubation patch* on its belly. The incubation patch

Two is the usual number of eggs in a clutch. The eggs can be white or tan.

lacks feathers and has blood vessels close to the surface, bringing warmth to the eggs as the parent presses against them.

A pigeon incubates its eggs.

The male sits on the nest from the middle of the morning until late afternoon, when his mate relieves him. When one bird leaves and the other takes over, the eggs are never left uncovered for more than two minutes. The eggs usually hatch fourteen to eighteen days after laying. The young bird has a special, sharp *egg tooth* on its beak that it uses to break through the shell. First, it makes one hole near the large end of the egg. Then, after resting, it pecks a neat circle and pushes with its shoulders to loosen the end of the shell. The little bird then uncoils its neck and struggles out of the shell about twenty-four hours after beginning the process.

At hatching, the young pigeons, called *squabs*, have only a thin coating of yellowish feathers. They use their paddlelike wings to position their unsteady bodies in

The young squabs have only a thin coat of yellow feathers.

the nest. Their eyes are closed, and they can barely lift their heads or open their mouths. But soon, they are hungry and ready to eat.

Pigeons feed their young with a special cheesy material called *crop milk* made by glands in the parents' crops. The hungry squab sticks its beak inside the parent's mouth, and the parent brings up a dose of crop milk. During the first week, the young birds feed three to four times a day. Then feeding slows down. Bit by bit, other foods such as seeds are added to the squabs' diet until they are eating only food brought by the parents in their second week of life.

A squab is fed crop milk by one of its parents.

The young birds grow fast, and their feathers come in quickly.

The squabs grow quickly, and by the age of twenty days, they are beginning to peck around the nest as if to feed themselves. Their feathers grow in quickly. When they are twenty-five to twenty-eight days old, they can fly short distances from the nest. For the next week, they continue to return to the nest. By the time they are seven weeks old, the young birds feed themselves completely, but they may stay near their parents. They spend more and more time in flocks and learn from the older birds where to find food and water. Bit by bit, they lose their attachment to their parents and become independent.

CHAPTER 4

Racing Home

EVER SINCE PEOPLE HAVE KEPT PIGEONS, they have been fascinated by the birds' amazing ability to find their way home. People have taken advantage of the homing instinct for long-distance communication since prehistoric times. According to the Bible, Noah sent out a raven to see if land had reemerged after the flood. The raven never returned. Then Noah sent out a dove (pigeon). It returned, apparently without finding land. Again he sent out a dove, and this one returned with an olive leaf, showing that land had finally reappeared.

In the middle of the fourth century B.C., the Greek philosopher and naturalist Aristotle wrote about pigeons, which were already being used as messengers. Such famous conquerors as Alexander the Great and Hannibal used pigeons to carry messages. The news of Napoleon's defeat at Waterloo arrived in England by carrier pigeon four days earlier than by horse and ship. Over eight hundred years ago, the ruler of Baghdad established a pigeon postal system, with post offices to which the pigeons were trained to fly.

Pigeons at home in the loft.

In Europe, pigeons were bred intensively for their ability to return home reliably, and by 1819, homing pigeons could fly up to two hundred miles in a day and had become important to newspapers as sources of the latest world events. In those days, there was no telegraph, telephone, or other fast means of rapid, long-distance communication. If a pigeon could bring the message in four or five hours, that was fast.

Pigeons in War

Homing pigeons almost certainly served during wartime in very early times, but the first record is from the armies of Julius Caesar during his conquest of Gaul, over two thousand years ago. From then on, these reliable birds served in many conflicts. One of their greatest services came during the Franco-Prussian War, when the city of Paris, France, was under siege from November 1870 to January 1871. The Parisians released balloons carrying pigeons over the city. The balloons carried the birds safely out of the besieged city. The birds then were taken to many European cities, including London, and released with messages to return to Paris.

During World War I, pigeons were vital for carrying messages to and from the front lines. Here, soldiers in France prepare pigeons to carry dispatches.
Courtesy Command Historian, U.S. Army Signal Corps

During this time, the technology for attaching messages to the birds was perfected. At first, the messages were tightly wrapped and then attached to the tail feathers with wax. Many of these messages never reached Paris. Later on, the messages were inserted into a hollow goose quill and tied to the pigeon's strongest tail feather. A great deal of information could be included in one message through an early form of microphotography. One miniature photograph could contain 2,500 messages, and a bird could carry twelve or more at a time. During the siege, over a million messages were brought into Paris by pigeon.

Even in the twentieth century, homing pigeons have played an important part during wartime. Cutting off communications is always a major goal in war, and when phone and telegraph lines are cut, pigeons can still fly through. In World War I, the Germans were so aware of the importance of pigeons that when they occupied Belgium and France, they ordered all pigeons destroyed.

Pigeons saved thousands of lives during World War II. British army aircraft carried pigeons. If the plane crashed at sea, a pigeon carrying a message giving the location of the crash was sent off, allowing rescuers to locate surviving crew members. Pigeons brought to Britain the first messages about the crucial Normandy Invasion and helped provide information about the location of German rocket launching sites. Thirty-two wartime pigeons received the Dickin Medal, awarded to animals that served humans heroically. One of these birds was an American-bred homing pigeon named G.I. Joe. He saved hundreds of British soldiers by carrying a message for bombers not to attack a position seized from the enemy. G.I. Joe arrived at the base just minutes before the bombers were to take off. After the war, G.I. Joe was flown to London to receive his honors.

The American army also used homing pigeons. At the height of World War II, over 3,000 men utilized 54,000 pigeons. These birds saw service in Asia, North

This pigeon is being released from its basket to carry a message to headquarters from a position on the battlefield hidden by a camouflage nest.
Courtesy Command Historian, U.S. Army Signal Corps

Africa, and Europe and saved countless lives with the messages they carried. For example, American pigeon hero Jungle Joe was only four months old when he was parachuted behind Japanese lines in Burma to carry messages from Allied scouts. They kept him for eight days while gathering information about the placement of enemy guns and troops, then released him with the data. Jungle Joe had to fly 225 miles through difficult winds and over some of Asia's steepest mountains. The vital information he carried allowed the Allies to capture a large portion of Burma.

Pigeons were very valuable as a quick way to send vital information. When the Allies were crossing a river and establishing a beachhead, they could tell where the enemy artillery was. They would mark the spot on a map overlay made from thin paper, then fold it into the message capsule of a pigeon. The pigeon could reach the Allied artillery emplacement in about ten minutes, while it would have taken a jeep over an hour to make the trip by land. The Allied artillery could then be aimed properly to knock out the enemy's fire. Many wartime homing pigeons were injured during their flights, yet they flew on, determined to reach home.

Racing for Fun

Racing pigeons has become a popular hobby—around the world, over a million people race pigeons in competition. It all started in Belgium near the beginning of the nineteenth century. The Belgians developed different strains of racing birds. These various types of pigeons were bred together to produce the racing pigeon of today. Some combinations produced fast flyers that could win short races, while other mixtures resulted in birds able to fly long distances at a consistently rapid pace. Pigeon racing is the national sport in Belgium today, with one man out of thirty participating.

These young Racing Homers, the Thoroughbreds of the bird world, are just learning about their home loft and how to find it.

The bird developed through this careful breeding is called the Racing Homer. Like the Thoroughbred horse and the Greyhound dog, the Racing Homer is a special breed, perfected for the purpose of flying swiftly and reliably home after being released up to five hundred miles away. Racing Homers are larger than ferals. They have especially large, sturdy breastbones for attachment of the big, strong chest muscles that power their flight.

Although the ability to head for home comes naturally to pigeons, especially Racing Homers, they still need some training for successful racing. The pigeons are housed in a small building called a *loft*. The loft may be on top of a building or on ground level. The loft is the pigeons' home, the place they head for when racing. There, they find a clean, dry, safe place with plenty of food and water and the companionship of the other birds in their flock. The loft features a ledge called the *landing board* and an opening for the birds to enter.

When a Racing Homer is five days old, the owner carefully slips a permanent leg band over one foot onto the leg. This band identifies each bird individually with a permanent identification number. The birds

Young birds on an early flight around the loft.

are separated from their parents at about twenty-five days of age and placed in the loft. From there, they can look out through the mesh windows and become familiar with the environment. Ten or fifteen days later, they are released from the loft for the first time. They fly about nearby. At first, each bird goes its own way. Gradually, they flock together and venture farther and farther from home. When they are three or four months old and have traveled four or five miles away on their own, they are ready to be carried away from home in baskets and released to find their way back.

The owner works up to a distance of fifty or sixty miles. Not all the birds make it—some have poor homing instincts, and others may be caught by predators such as wild falcons. If a pigeon fancier starts out with fifty birds, he may have about thirty-five left when racing season begins.

Alan Harriman lets his pigeons loose to find their way home on a trial race.

Pigeons in their "basket" await release.

The Race

Pigeon racing is different from more familiar kinds of racing. Instead of all the competitors' starting and finishing in the same place, the birds all start together but each bird flies to its home loft. Determining the winners in such a race is a bit complicated. Before a fancier races his birds, the exact air distance, calculated to the one-thousandth of a kilometer, from his loft to each of the race starting points used in his area is measured and recorded. That way, race officials establish the official distance the birds will have to fly to return home.

The day before a race, each owner separates his male and female birds, puts them in carrying containers, and takes them to a central location. He also brings along his special race clock.

At the prerace gathering, temporary leg bands called counterbands are slipped onto the birds' unbanded legs. The counterband has each bird's permanent identification number as well as a special number for the race. All the race clocks are synchronized so they will all record time identically. Then all the birds are driven to the starting point, where they are released together at a predetermined moment.

Two styles of race clock.

Alan Harriman removes the counterband from a pigeon that has returned home during a race.

Each owner has to keep an eye out for his birds, starting as early as he thinks they might make it home. At this point, the training of the birds can be just as important as their speed. A speedy bird that lands in a tree near the loft is no good—the bird must come to the loft right away so the owner can capture it.

The bird lands on the landing board and enters the trap, a small cagelike compartment of the loft. After the pigeon enters the trap, the owner closes the door and captures the bird. Once he has the bird in hand, he removes the counterband and inserts it into a special capsule that fits into a hole in his race clock. He then turns the crank on the clock, which stamps the bird's arrival time on a paper tape so there is an official record of when each bird returned home. Then he waits for the next bird. The counterbands are held in order inside the clock so they can be matched to the tape showing arrival times.

A race clock opened up to show how it works. In the lower right is the roll of paper that is stamped with the arrival time of each bird. Behind it and to the left is the cylinder with holes in it that receives the capsules containing the counterbands.

Alan is about to insert the counterband into the clock. After he does so, he will wind the lever behind so the clock will stamp the time on the paper and the cylinder will rotate, ready to receive the next counterband.

No one knows who has won the race until all the pigeon owners have gathered with their clocks after the race is over. A race official opens all the clocks and records the times of arrival of the birds that made it home. Then the speed of each bird is measured in yards per minute. The fastest bird is the winner, and the top three all get diplomas showing their race placement and how fast they flew. Fifty miles per hour is considered a fast pace.

The first race of the season is about a hundred miles long, perhaps twice as far as young birds have flown toward home before. But the birds find their way home anyway, even over unfamiliar territory. Races may be up to five hundred miles long, or even a little longer. On longer races, many birds may never make it back to their home loft.

Most racing pigeon fanciers race their birds as a hobby. But in some parts of the country, racing can bring in big money. Serious fanciers who race their birds may pay as much as $2,500 for just one untried young bird!

The Mystery of Homing

Even though many scientists have devoted their careers to studying this amazing talent, we still aren't sure of all the factors that enter into how pigeons navigate. While modern races are usually five hundred miles or less, pigeons can be trained to return home from distances of over a thousand miles. How do they do it?

Even on a partially cloudy day, a pigeon can use the sun to help it find its way home.

Beginning in the 1940s, scientists began to study this question seriously. They learned that birds such as pigeons can use the location of the sun in the sky as a guide. Since the sun's position changes as the day progresses, the birds also must have a way of adjusting to that change by using an internal sense of the passage of time. Pigeons also use landmarks to find home, but apparently not until they are within nine to twelve miles of their home loft.

Using the sun as a guide, however, can't be the whole answer. Even if skies are cloudy, pigeons released far from home will head in the right direction. Since the 1880s, a few scientists suspected that pigeons could sense the earth's magnetic field and use it to navigate. But for years, this idea was rejected. Then, in the early 1970s, William Keeton of Cornell University showed that pigeons can use magnetism to navigate. He trained pigeons to return home, then attached tiny magnets to the wings of some birds and nonmagnetic bars to the wings of others. Five of seven birds with the nonmagnetic bars headed right for home. But the birds wearing magnets scattered

Wherever they roam, pigeons can find their way home again.

randomly when released. Other scientists showed that magnetically confused pigeons could still find their way home if the sun was out but got lost when it was cloudy.

Respecting Pigeons

Our relationships with pigeons have been complicated over the thousands of years that these adaptable birds have associated with people. They have provided us with a tasty and valuable source of meat and have enabled us to have long-distance communication before we had telegraph, airplanes, and satellites to speed messages through the air. Pigeons have given us a way to express our competitive urges, through shows based on beauty and through races that test the homing instinct and flying speed. In addition, pigeons have proved to be loyal and friendly pets.

Pigeons have also annoyed us by leaving their abundant and corrosive droppings on public buildings and statues. Their droppings and nesting material can clog rain gutters, and some people worry about the diseases they may transmit to people. Although many people may not appreciate city pigeons, these birds are almost certainly here to stay—they are too adaptable, intelligent, and hardy to get rid of easily.

Meanwhile, those who appreciate pigeons can watch their graceful flight and listen to their soothing cooing, in this way enjoying a touch of wildness in the depths of even the most human-dominated landscapes.

A beautiful white Jacobin.

Glossary

cere—A piece of skin growing over part of a pigeon's beak.

counterband—A band slipped onto a Racing Homer's leg before a race. The counterband records the bird's permanent ID number and its race ID number.

crop milk—A cheesy liquid made in the parent pigeons' throats that the birds use to feed their young.

dove—Generally the smaller species in the pigeon family.

egg tooth—A temporary tooth on the beak of a young bird used to break its way out of the egg.

Fantail—A pigeon breed with a graceful, upright tail

that has more than the normal number of feathers.

feral—Animals living in the wild, whose ancestors were domesticated.

Giant Runt—A breed of pigeon developed for its meat; it can weigh more than 3$^1/_2$ pounds.

gizzard—A part of the throat of a bird. It has muscular walls that contains grit used to help grind up the bird's food.

incubation patch—A bare area on the breast of parent birds that is well supplied with blood vessels. The incubation patch provides warmth to eggs as they are incubated.

landing board—A board in front of the trap where Racing Homers land.

loft—The building which houses pigeons.

race clock—The special clock owned by every person

with racing birds, used to time the arrival time home of Racing Homers.

rock dove—The wild ancestor of domesticated pigeons.

Roller—A breed of pigeon that performs acrobatic feats as it flies.

squab—A young pigeon.

trap—The small cagelike compartment of the loft. The Racing Homer enters the trap when it returns at the end of a race.

Tumbler—A breed of pigeon that does backward somersaults in the air.

White King—A large breed of pigeon bred for eating.

Index

Italics refer to illustrations or captions.

$16.00

DATE			